Timeline of American Pioneers

1803–1806
Lewis and Clark Expedition to the Pacific coast.

1828
Construction begins on the Baltimore and Ohio Railroad, one of the first U.S. railroads. Andrew Jackson, advocate of western expansion, is elected president of the United States.

1812–1814
War between the United States and Great Britain.

1837
John Deere patents the steel plow.

1800
Population of the United States recorded as 5,308,483.

1818
The United States and Great Britain agree to joint occupancy of Oregon country.

1811
John Jacob Astor establishes a trading post in Oregon.

1830
Joseph Smith founds the Mormon church.

1845
The Lone Star Republic enters the Union as the state of Texas.

1861–1865
The Civil War.

1848
Gold is discovered in California, leading to the 1849–1850 gold rush.

1842–1845
John Frémont maps the West.

1843
First large wagon train crosses to Oregon.

1860
The first ride of the Pony Express delivers letters from Missouri to California in ten days.

1836
The Lone Star Republic (Texas) becomes independent from Mexico.

1846
California becomes independent from Mexico as the Bear Flag Republic.

1869
The first U.S. transcontinental railroad is completed.

Map of the Western Trails

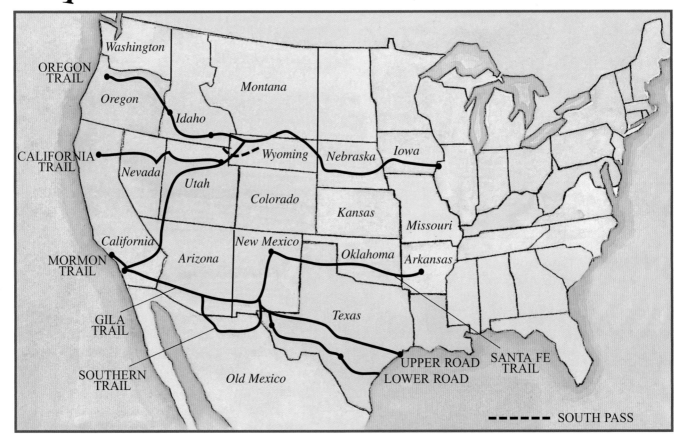

OREGON TRAIL

Washington

Oregon

Idaho

Montana

CALIFORNIA TRAIL

Nevada

Utah

Wyoming

Nebraska

Iowa

Colorado

Kansas

Missouri

California

New Mexico

Oklahoma

Arkansas

MORMON TRAIL

Arizona

Texas

GILA TRAIL

SOUTHERN TRAIL

Old Mexico

UPPER ROAD

LOWER ROAD

SANTA FE TRAIL

- - - - - SOUTH PASS

The Way West

The discovery of the South Pass—the only easy way to cross the Rockies—changed the way that the people of the United States thought about the North American continent and their place in it. Until this discovery, the far West had seemed too distant for most Americans to consider exploring. Then in the 1830s, word spread that the Pacific regions, including Oregon (the Columbia area to which Britain had a claim) and California (which belonged to Mexico) were lands of opportunity where fortunes could be made. Many U.S. citizens were suddenly eager to settle there. They believed it was their nation's destiny to fill the continent from coast to coast with U.S. citizens.

Author:

Jacqueline Morley studied English at Oxford University. She has taught English and history and has a special interest in the history of everyday life. She is the author of numerous children's books, including award-winning historical nonfiction for children.

Artist:

David Antram was born in Brighton, England, in 1958. He studied at Eastbourne College of Art and then worked in advertising for fifteen years before becoming a full-time artist. He has illustrated many children's nonfiction books.

Series Creator:

David Salariya was born in Dundee, Scotland. He has illustrated a wide range of books and has created and designed many new series for publishers both in the UK and overseas. In 1989, he established The Salariya Book Company. He lives in Brighton with his wife, illustrator Shirley Willis, and their son Jonathan.

Editors:

Karen Barker Smith
Stephanie Cole

© The Salariya Book Company Ltd MMXIII
No part of this publication may be reproduced in whole or in part, or stored in a retrieval system, or transmitted in any form or by any means, electronic, mechanical, photocopying, recording, or otherwise, without written permission of the publisher. For information regarding permission, write to the copyright holder.

Published in Great Britain in 2013 by
The Salariya Book Company Ltd
25 Marlborough Place, Brighton BN1 1UB

ISBN-13: 978-0-531-27500-9 (lib. bdg.)   978-0-531-28025-6 (pbk.)

All rights reserved.
Published in 2013 in the United States
by Franklin Watts
An imprint of Scholastic Inc.
Published simultaneously in Canada.

A CIP catalog record for this book is available
from the Library of Congress.

Printed and bound in China.
Printed on paper from sustainable sources.
1 2 3 4 5 6 7 8 9 10 R 22 21 20 19 18 17 16 15 14 13

SCHOLASTIC, FRANKLIN WATTS, and associated logos are trademarks and/or registered trademarks of Scholastic Inc.

You Wouldn't Want to Be an American Pioneer!

American Pioneer!

Watch out for those buffalo!

A Wilderness You'd Rather Not Tame

Written by
Jacqueline Morley

Illustrated by
David Antram

Created and designed by
David Salariya

Franklin Watts®
An Imprint of Scholastic Inc.
NEW YORK • TORONTO • LONDON • AUCKLAND • SYDNEY
MEXICO CITY • NEW DELHI • HONG KONG
DANBURY, CONNECTICUT

Contents

Introduction

In the 1840s, most people of the United States live near the eastern coast of North America. This is the only known region of the continent. As a farmer, you have no idea what the rest of the land is like. You are willing to cross over two-thirds of the continent to find out, though.

Why do you plan to go west? Traders who have sailed around North America to the other side of the continent are saying that the West Coast is a wonderful place. There is good soil and plenty of land available to farm, and you can be your own boss. You do not have the time or money for a long sea voyage, so you are planning to join hundreds of other pioneer families who want to journey west over land to Oregon. You know hardly anything about the dangers you are about to face — huge mountains, lack of food and water, disease, scary animals, and strange insects. If you knew, you certainly wouldn't want to be an American pioneer!

Go West and Get Rich!

You will not be the first to go west over land. A few explorers and fur trappers have made the trip already. They say it is tough but possible. What you need is a good strong wagon, packed with everything for the journey. You fill your wagon with enough goods to last at least five months: sacks of beans, flour, and dried fruit; barrels of bacon, coffee, and sugar; clothes, bedding, tents, tools, guns, cooking equipment, medicine, soap, and candles. With all that on board, there is hardly room for people. It is important not to take more than your animals can pull. If they get worn out, you will never make it to your destination.

If I were him, I'd be tempted to leave that clock behind!

Decisions, Decisions...

DEVELOPERS visit towns to tell of the wonders of Oregon, the West Coast paradise where farming is "easy."

POLITICIANS tell you to go west for your country's sake — if Americans don't settle in Oregon, the British will. You have to sell your farm to finance the trip.

NOT EVERYONE thinks that traveling over 2,000 miles (3,200 km) through the unknown is a good idea. Relatives weep as you set off.

7

Ganging Up – Don't Travel Alone!

Stock Up on Supplies

THE TOWN OF INDEPENDENCE specializes in equipping wagon trains. If there is anything you forgot to pack or did not realize you would need, you can buy it here. Prices are high, though.

Pioneer families take their wagons and meet at a convenient point: Independence, Missouri, the westernmost U.S. town. The pioneers form "trains" of wagons traveling together for safety. The land they have to cross belongs to native tribes of people called Indians. They might be dangerous — who knows?

Sugar

Coffee

Flour

Guns

Bedding

Axe

Mallet

Saw

Spring is the only time to start the long journey west, so the town is packed with people. Everyone is excited, and no one knows what to expect. You hear all sorts of rumors about lack of water in the rivers, floods, and Indian attacks. Most wagon trains hire a guide, such as a fur trapper who has been west and knows at least part of the route.

Handy Hint

Take a "walking larder" with you — some live animals that you can kill and eat on the journey. Buy them at Independence.

Are you sure you know the way?

Better than you, that's for sure!

Into the Unknown

The pioneer families set off in a long line of wagons. Wagon drivers race to get to the front of the line to avoid the dust stirred up by other wagons. Going too fast exhausts the oxen and mules that pull the wagons. Two miles an hour (3.2 kph) is all they can do comfortably. It is not long before people are bickering.

No one can agree when to stop for a rest, where to camp, or who should keep watch at night. It is soon clear that rules and a daily routine will have to be established. Don't grumble when you are woken at dawn to get moving, and don't sneak off when it is your turn for guard duty at night.

Stop Fighting!

THE MEN of the wagon train elect officers to keep order, settle disputes, and punish those who disobey the rules. The women are not allowed to help make these decisions.

Fell asleep on guard duty, did you?!

As an elected officer, I will organize guard duty this evening!

Handy Hint

Don't start your journey too early in the year, or there won't be enough grass growing to feed your animals. Don't leave too late, though, or you won't get over the mountains before they are blocked by snow.

Wet and Weary

Sandstorms

SAND IN YOUR FACE. West winds whip the dry, sandy soil into clouds of stinging dust.

Grass, grass, and more grass — that's all you see for at least two months, as the wagons follow the muddy Platte River across an endless plain. The journey, which was fun at first, gets boring and exhausting. The Sun beats down, and there is not a single tree for shade. Suddenly, out of nowhere, black clouds pile up to create violent storms. Lightning flashes make the animals bolt. Wind rips the wagon covers off and blows away the tents. In minutes, everyone is drenched, and the campsite becomes a sea of mud.

SORE EYES. The sand makes your eyes sting and your eyelids swell up. Your lips get puffed and split.

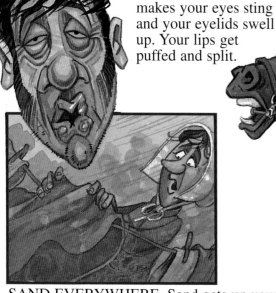

SAND EVERYWHERE. Sand gets up your nose and down your throat, into your food and bedding, and all over your clean clothes.

Handy Hint

Hold an umbrella over your pot if you need to keep cooking in the rain.

Run for it!

I think someone left a window open.

Injured Animals

One of your oxen is lame. It has trodden on a cactus spine, and its hoof is infected. Cut out the bad flesh and seal the wound with hot tar.

Make the ox a protective shoe out of buffalo skin and tie it on.

Watch Out – Indians!

People You Will Meet

The vast grassland you are crossing, known as the Great Plains, is the home of the Plains Indians. They live by hunting buffalo.

SIOUX. They are one of the most powerful of the Plains Indian tribes.

Sooner or later you will come across Indians. They spend their time hunting, so they are experts with bows and arrows, and you have heard stories about how fierce they are. They are fascinated by your odd-looking clothes and tools. Some of the Plains tribes have made an agreement with the U.S. government. They will let the wagons pass safely, and in return they can charge a toll. If you don't pay up, you can't expect the Indians to keep their side of the bargain.

CHINOOKS. You will meet this tribe, who flatten their heads, at the end of your journey.

BLACKFEET. They don't put up with any nonsense. Other Plains Indians are afraid of them.

PAWNEE. They are used to meeting white settlers and have been known to take horses in return for letting you cross their land.

YOU will also meet the Mandans, Shoshone, Nez Perce, and many more tribes. Remember: it is their land you're crossing, so be polite to them.

14

Stampede!

If you hear a noise like thunder from the plains above the river, watch out! This sound is the pounding hooves of a herd of buffalo galloping your way. Something has made these huge animals panic, and now nothing can stop them. You must try to get the wagons out of the way before they are crushed in the stampede. Normally the buffalo graze peacefully on the plains. Plains Indians rely on the buffalo for everything they need — they eat almost nothing else and use the hides to make clothes and tents. There are huge herds of buffalo in North America at the moment, but your fellow pioneers are killing an awful lot of them.

Buffalo Problems

BUFFALO DRINKING. Buffalo coming to drink make deep ruts in the river banks. This gives the wagons such a bumpy ride that wheels come off.

PANIC! A stampeding herd of buffalo can make your animals bolt off in panic too. They could break their legs or trample people.

HARD TARGET. Unless you know the right spot to hit, it is difficult to kill a buffalo. Indians can fell one with a single arrow.

Mealtimes – Feeling Queasy?

The women do the cooking, and it is a thankless job. There is no tap water, no tables, and nothing to cook on until a fire has been lit. Flying insects drop into the cooking pot. You and your family are fed up with rancid bacon and homemade bread that is full of sand. If you are lucky and kill a buffalo, you'll have more fresh meat than you can cope with. Then you should do as the Indians do. Cut the leftover meat into strips and dry it out. Packed into a barrel, the dry meat (called jerky) will keep for a long time, and you can boil it later.

THIRSTY? After traveling in the Sun all day, you won't mind drinking muddy river water. That odd flavor is probably buffalo urine.

WELLS. Dig a well to reach underground water. You will pass lots of wells dug by previous pioneers.

GERMS! Well water might taste better, but the wells contain germs from other wagoners. Watch for an upset stomach!

DISEASE. Cholera, a deadly fever, can be caught from infected water. You will pass lots of graves of cholera victims.

HUNGRY? What could be worse than eating nothing but dried meat, beans, and boiled flour? How about eating them after they've spoiled! The only thing worse is not having anything left to eat at all.

19

Sink or Swim — River Crossings

Lots of people are drowned trying to cross rivers. Many pioneers cannot swim because swimming wasn't taught at school. You have to get over the rivers, and there aren't any bridges. Sometimes there is a ford — a place where the water is shallow enough for the wagons to be led across.

Fording is dangerous, though. The wagons are linked by chains for safety, but strong currents could sweep a wagon sideways. If the chain snaps, the wagon could overturn and be carried away downstream.

Too Deep to Ford?

FELL TREES and make a raft big enough to carry each wagon.

ANIMALS swim or cross by raft. If they panic, they might upset the raft.

NO TREES? Cover the base of the wagon with buffalo skins and float it over.

BE CAREFUL. Up to ninety wagoners drown each year.

At the Fort

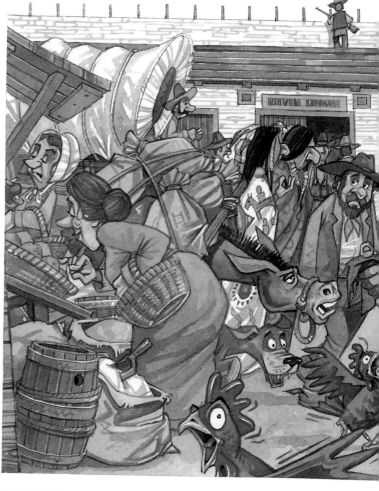

Your food is running out, your wagon is falling to bits, and your animals look as though they cannot last another day. There are mountains in the distance that you have to cross. You would never manage all this without a stop at Fort Laramie. This fortified enclosure, far out in the wilds, belongs to the American Fur Company. Officials who buy furs from trappers and Indians live here. You can buy food at the fort's store (if there is any food to spare) and give yourself and your animals a few days' rest.

Lots to Do at the Fort

MENDING. You can borrow tools from the fort's carpentry workshop and give your wagon a good overhaul.

WASHING. Your smelly clothes and blankets get a real scrub at last. Women spend all day at it.

BUYING. You haggle with the storekeeper over his prices, but it doesn't work. He has plenty of other customers.

Handy Hint

Trade your tired animals in for fresh ones. Your old beasts will rest and be sold later.

LISTENING. You will hear lots of different advice about the best route to take across the Rocky Mountains.

RELAXING. There is nothing to worry about for a few days, so you have a dance around the campfire at night.

SLEEPING. You can sleep soundly at night (and all day too if you need to) because there is good security around the fort.

Done In and Done For

Why Your Animals Might Not Make It:

re mules or oxen best at pulling wagons? Pioneers argue endlessly over this before making their choice. Mules walk faster, but oxen can pull more weight — and they are nicer to eat if you are starving. Whichever you choose, remember that your life depends on them. If you cannot keep your wagon moving, you will be stranded in the wilderness at the mercy of wolves, bears, and hostile tribes.

NOTHING TO EAT. If you see no grass for days, oxen will suffer more than mules. Mules will eat anything.

NOTHING TO DRINK. Lack of water, or drinking from a pool that is alkaline, can kill your animals.

WALKED TO DEATH. Pulling a wagon for months, over mountains and plains, your beasts might finally sink to their knees and never get up.

Now What?

THE WAGON TRAIN must keep going. If no one has animals to lend you, it will leave you behind.

WAIT by the trail and see if the next train has spare animals.

SET OFF walking and hope that you are not far from another fort.

Handy Hint

To save your animals, lighten their load. Throw all non-essential items out of your wagon.

Don't stop now — we'll be goners for sure!

The Last Lap
Delays to Your Journey

You must reach the West Coast by October, before bad weather sets in and snow blocks the Rockies. After the Rockies are parched, dusty plains, more mountains, and the Columbia River, with rapids and a gorge you must navigate by raft. If you don't drown in the Columbia, you might die from one of the illnesses that plague the pioneers. Months of eating food lacking in vitamin C causes scurvy, with the exhaustion, bleeding gums, and aching limbs that disease brings. Deadly "mountain fever" is carried by a bloodsucking tick.

SLOPES too steep to climb. You have to make a pulley to haul the wagons up.

BANKS AND GULLIES. Precious time is lost getting down these obstacles. Animals have to be lowered on ropes.

CLIFFS. Guiding the wagons along the narrow mountain passes or precipices is slow and dangerous.

SLOW PROGRESS. By now, your animals are too weak to go faster.

RAPIDS. The rafts must be unloaded. For a fee, Indians might carry the baggage around.

OBSTACLES. The route might be blocked by giant boulders, which you have to haul aside.

Journey's End

Your Own Piece of Oregon

You have reached Oregon at last! You claim some land, but it is covered in trees. There is no home waiting for you, so you have to build one. There are no fields to farm — you must clear the trees before you can plant anything.

THE SOIL must be good since so many trees grow well in it. It's a pity they are in the way!

CHOP CHOP. You spend your days felling trees.

HEAVE! The oxen don't get a rest either.

SLASH AND BURN. You tackle the undergrowth by hacking at it and setting it on fire.

Whose idea was this pioneer thing anyway?

First you make a log cabin for shelter. Pioneers join forces to do the heavy work of hauling logs into place and setting up the roof. Then, when you have plowed the land you have cleared, you can begin a lifetime of hard work on it.

Handy Hint

Don't throw out the old tents and wagon cloth. Use them to make clothes and mattress covers.

SNAP!

SNAP!

Watch out!

Glossary

Alkaline water Water in which certain mineral salts are found. Very alkaline water can be poisonous.

Buffalo A type of large wild cattle. In the 19th century, vast herds of buffalo roamed the central plains of North America.

Cholera A fever that can kill a person in 24 hours. It is caught by contact with an infected person or through contaminated food or water.

Fort A building with strong outer walls and watchtowers. The forts in North America were also supply depots and trading places for trappers, fur-company officials, and wagoners.

Gully A steep-sided channel with a stream running through it.

Indians The old term for the native peoples of America. These people are now called American Indians or Native Americans.

Log cabin A small house with walls made of horizontally laid logs.

Oregon A large area of northwest North America, known after the late 18th century as Oregon Country. Both Britain and the United States claimed it as theirs and had competing fur companies there. Oregon became a state in 1859.

Pioneer A person who leads the way into unknown country.

Precipice A very steep face of a rock, cliff, or mountain.

Sandstorm Sand hurled through the air by strong winds.

Scurvy An illness caused by not eating enough vitamin C.

Stampede A herd of cattle panicked into galloping together.

Tick A tiny, bloodsucking creature that attaches itself, by its mouth, to the skin of humans and other animals.

Toll A payment, in money or goods, for the right to pass through an area of land.

Trappers Men who lived in the wilds of North America, where beavers were plentiful, in order to trap them for their furs. Trappers were also known as mountain men.

Index

Why Go West?

There are many factors that contributed to the American pioneers' decision to head west. Here are just a few them:

Financial Woes

In 1837, the nation suffered its first major financial collapse. It was the result of irresponsible money and banking policies and unwise buying and selling of public lands during the Andrew Jackson administration. During May of 1837, New York's major banks failed, creating panic that led to more banks closing all over the country. The depression that followed caused agricultural prices to plummet. Farm surpluses clogged the produce markets, and farmers could not meet the mortgage payments on their land. These farmers headed for free land on the West Coast.

Epidemics

Health epidemics also drove people to the West. In the East, diseases such as typhoid, dysentery, tuberculosis, scarlet fever, and malaria were the leading causes of death. Yellow fever so devastated the population of New Orleans and settlements along the Mississippi River to the north that the regional death rate exceeded the birth rate for nearly a century. In the 1830s, a cholera epidemic began in Asia. It then rampaged through Europe, came across the Atlantic on passenger ships, struck the East Coast, and spread inland. The disease raged for almost two decades, killing some 30,000 people in 1850 alone.

The Civil War

The Civil War sent yet another wave of pioneers to the West. In the aftermath of the war, thousands of people wanted to escape their devastated homes. They viewed the West as a place where they could achieve health, wealth, and happiness.

Top American Pioneers

Lewis and Clark

In 1803, French emperor Napoleon Bonaparte sold the huge Louisiana Territory to the United States. President Thomas Jefferson hoped the Louisiana Purchase would provide an easy trade route to the Pacific coast. He chose two army officers, Meriwether Lewis and William Clark, to lead an expedition. They set off up the Missouri River in 1804. After many months of dangerous travel (horses fell over cliffs and food was running out), the expedition reached the Pacific Ocean on November 15, 1805.

On June 14, 1805, Lewis escaped from a grizzly bear by swimming a river.

Lewis and Clark made a good team. Lewis was a scholar, interested in scientific observation. He was a brilliant organizer, and a quiet and rather reserved man. The more outgoing Clark was an excellent second-in-command. Lewis later became governor of Louisiana Territory.

The route found by Lewis and Clark was far too difficult to be used for regular travel. In February 1824, a party of trappers led by Jedediah Smith was traveling west when snow blocked their way. A Crow Indian told them of a more southerly route through the mountains. Smith and his party realized this was the ideal route to the West. They called it the South Pass.

John Charles Frémont

Tales of fortunes to be made in the West soon spread, and many people set out on the dangerous journey. But there were no maps or marked routes. In 1842, the U.S. government appointed army surveyor John Frémont to map out the best routes. Frémont's nickname was the Great Pathfinder. His books about his expedition sold in huge numbers. He climbed what he thought was the highest peak in the Rockies, planting the American flag on the summit. It was a wonderful gesture, but he had chosen the wrong peak—others are higher!

In 1845, Frémont's mapping work was interrupted by war between the United States and Mexico. The unequal conflict didn't last long. Mexico lost California, which became the 31st state of the United States. Frémont was appointed military governor. He became a millionaire after the gold rush of 1848, and was even nominated for the presidency in 1856.

Daniel Boone

Daniel Boone was an explorer known for his trailblazing through the American frontier. He went with British general Edward Braddock to Fort Duquesne in 1755. He helped make the Wilderness Road, a major road through the Kentucky Territory, and named several towns after himself, such as Boonesborough, Kentucky.

Did You Know?

- Brigham Young led 70,000 Mormons along the **Mormon Trail** from 1846 to 1869 to escape religious persecution.
- The **Overland Trail** (also known as the Overland Stage Line) was a stagecoach and wagon train route in the American West during the 1800s.
- The **California Trail** was the main route to the Golden State of California. More than 250,000 gold seekers and farmers followed that trail in hopes of finding riches and better land to farm.
- The **Cherokee Trail**, also known as the Trappers' Trail, was established in 1849 by a wagon train headed for the goldfields in California.